MAKE YOUR OWN
MONEY

MAKE *YOUR* OWN
MONEY

HOW KIDS CAN

EARN
IT

SAVE
IT

SPEND
IT

AND
DREAM
BIG

WITH *Danny Dollar,* THE *King* OF *Cha-Ching*

TY ALLAN JACKSON

ILLUSTRATED BY
NICOLE MILES

Storey Publishing

The mission of Storey Publishing is to serve our customers by publishing practical information that encourages personal independence in harmony with the environment.

Edited by Deanna F. Cook, Hannah Fries, and Sarah Guare
Art direction and book design by Ash Austin
Text production by Jennifer Jepson Smith
Indexed by Christine R. Lindemer, Boston Road Communications
Cover and interior illustrations by © Nicole Miles
Additional illustrations by Ash Austin © Storey Publishing, LLC, 4, 5 (presidents), 8–9 (all ex. Noogie), 10 (dollar), 26–27 (all ex. background), 34–35 (all ex. Uncle Earl), 39 t.r.

Text © 2021 by Ty Allan Jackson

Storey Publishing
210 MASS MoCA Way
North Adams, MA 01247
storey.com

Printed in China by R.R. Donnelley
10 9 8 7 6 5 4 3 2 1

LIBRARY OF CONGRESS CATALOGING-IN-PUBLICATION DATA ON FILE

To my Uncle Earl Taylor &
Uncle Schimeon Frederick

· ·

Thanks for showing me all I needed
to know about what really matters.

CONT

ENTS

MEET
DANNY DOLLAR

SAY IT WITH ME, WILL YA?

MONEY!
MOOOONN
NNNNNEE
EEEEYYYYY!

Hey! Thanks for picking up this book! You have no idea how much it means to me that you're reading it. After all, this book is for you! Yeah, I know, millions of other kids will read it. But, believe it or not, this book is for them, too. This book is for EVERYONE, and that's because it's about something that each and every one of us needs to know about: **MONEY!** Money is kinda one of those things that everyone needs, like oxygen and chocolate chip cookies. In other words, it's pretty darn important.

SO . . . MONEY!

It's my favorite word. It just rolls off the tongue.

To me there isn't a sweeter word in the English language. *Cookie* is a distant second. Obviously, I have a thing for cookies, but let's stay focused . . .

Where was I? . . . **OH, YEAH. MONEY!**

I just love money. And when I say I love it, I don't mean that I just love having it. Of course, everyone loves to have money. **DUH!** But I love everything about it. I love the history of money. The science of money. I like that weird smell of money . . .

Oops. I'm just blabbing on and on, and I haven't even introduced myself. **My name is Danny. Danny Dollar.** Some call me the King of Cha-Ching or Dan the Man with the Plan. Either way, when it comes to knowing anything (and I mean *anything*) about money, I'm your guy.

How do I know so much about money? Well, it all started when I was about five years old. My Uncle Earl would come over and watch football every Sunday with my dad. As soon as he walked in, he'd reach into his pocket, pull out two five-dollar bills, and give one to me and one to my sister. *CHA-CHING!* As you could imagine, I was super happy when football season came around. First time he handed me the five spot, he patted me on the head and said, **"Danny, make it grow."**

DANNY, MAKE IT GROW.

Ever since Uncle Earl challenged me, all I could think about was how to make money and how to make it grow.

Now, you might be saying to yourself that money isn't that complicated. My parents stick a card into a machine and money comes out. We spend it on stuff, *END OF STORY.* Oh, my friend! I am so glad you picked up this book, because money is so much more than something that you spend, and while it can come out of an ATM machine, that's just one tiny part of the awesomeness of money.

So I want you to get comfy, get a snack or beverage if you like, and prepare to learn more about money than that Monopoly dude with the monocle knows. You know, the guy with the eye thingy . . . never mind.

Okay, in this book, we're going to learn everything about money! Where it came from. How you can earn it and make it grow. How to start your own business even though you may not be old enough to drive a car. How to spend it wisely. How to invest it or donate it. (Don't worry, I'll explain what investing means.) Because you can make money at any age! Not as a doctor, lawyer, or anything like that. But you can become an *entrepreneur* right now and start minding your own business, literally! (Yep, I'll explain what an entrepreneur is, too.)

Danny Dollar

The King of Cha-Ching

READY? TURN THE PAGE AND
LET'S GET OUR CHA-CHING ON!

WHAT IS MONEY?

Cash, currency, moolah, dough, cabbage, bread, paper, Benjamins, bucks . . . we can call money all sorts of things. But at the end of the day, money is money. But what exactly *is* money? I'm glad you asked!

At some point in life, each of us is introduced to money. We probably don't remember that first introduction, but I'm guessing that as young children, most of us saw mom or dad hand someone a bill and receive something in return: a snack, a book, a watch, something that was exchanged for the money. And that's basically what money is: something you exchange for something else.

I recall being about four years old and going grocery shopping with my mom. I was sitting in the shopping cart at the local supermarket trying to grab and toss as many snacks into the cart as possible. Mom said, **"You can only have one treat,"** and handed me $1.00. I picked out a bag of chips that cost $1.79.

Mom said, **"That's too much money, honey. Find something under $1.00."**

I wasn't sure why my dollar wasn't enough for the chips. Then I grabbed a carton of ice cream for $2.99. Mom said, **"Danny, that's even more money than the chips. You have to pick something under $1.00."** She explained that everything has value, including the carton of ice cream and chips, and pointed to the posted prices.

EVERYTHING HAS VALUE.

Then I saw a mound of apples. I love apples! They were only $0.69. Less than a dollar! Mom winked at me and said, **"Nice job, Danny. Now you got it."**

We went to the cashier. I gave the cashier my buck. She handed me 31 cents, and on the way home, I sat in my booster seat and proudly ate my apple. That's my first memory of the value of money.

"PICK ONE TREAT THAT'S UNDER $1.00"

$1.79 $0.69 ea. $0.32 $2.99 $3

Usually money is exchanged for a GOOD or a SERVICE. A good is an item, like an apple, a pair of sneakers, a hat, a phone—you know, a thing. A service is a job that someone does for someone else, like babysit, clean teeth, build a house, or a fix a car. We'll talk more about goods and services in the next chapter.

Another word for exchanging goods and services is BARTERING. Back in the old days, paper money and coins didn't exist. Instead, people exchanged stuff like animals, shells, and even salt! There were many different forms of exchange. The problem was how to figure out the value of what you were exchanging. Think about it: What kind of animal would you exchange for an ice cream cone? How many shells would your video game cost? How many pounds of salt would it take to purchase a new skateboard? It was really hard to figure out how much something was worth. So paper money and coins were created and given a measure of value. GENIUS! Now you can know for sure that a haircut will cost you 15 bucks or a hamburger will cost you $4.50. For the record, my mom's burgers are worth like a million dollars. They're so yummy!

MONEY
AROUND THE WORLD

Pretty much the whole world agreed on this value system called money. Pretty awesome! Different countries all have different types of money. In the United States, we use dollars and cents. But in different parts of the world, money looks like this:

CANADIAN DOLLAR

EUROPEAN EURO

JAPANESE YEN

SOUTH AFRICAN RAND

BRITISH POUND

MEXICAN PESO

GEORGE WASHINGTON

As for U.S. money, all forms of our currency feature a president or dynamic leader.

Notice something similar about everyone depicted on paper money? They're all old white guys? Nothing against old white guys, but how come there are no women and no one from a different race or ethnicity?

ABRAHAM LINCOLN

BUT HOLD UP! President Andrew Jackson is on the 20-dollar bill right now, but in the not-too-distant future, his face might be replaced with that of the most famous conductor of the Underground Railroad, Harriet Tubman. That would be cool.

ALEXANDER HAMILTON

ANDREW JACKSON

BENJAMIN FRANKLIN

WHO ELSE WOULD YOU LIKE TO SEE ON A DOLLAR BILL? HOW ABOUT THESE PEOPLE?

MARTIN LUTHER KING, JR.

ROSA PARKS

FREDERICK DOUGLASS

SONIA SOTOMAYOR

DID YOU KNOW?

There are two historical figures featured on U.S. bills who were never president of the United States: Benjamin Franklin on the 100-dollar bill, and Alexander Hamilton on the 10-dollar bill.

BUREAU OF ENGRAVING AND PRINTING

WHERE IS **MONEY MADE?**

For the record, money does not grow on trees. If it did, I would be a lumberjack! **TIMBER!**

But if you wanna be technical about it, the stuff money is printed on *is* grown. Paper money is made up of 75 percent cotton and 25 percent linen. Both cotton and linen (or flax) come from plants, not trees!

Paper money is made at the Bureau of Engraving and Printing, which is run by the federal government. There are two locations, one in Washington, D.C., and another in Fort Worth, Texas. They print about 541 million bucks a day! That's right: $541,000,000. WOW! That's over 197 *billion* dollars a year! You would need a piggy bank the size of Yankee Stadium to hold that much CHA-CHING.

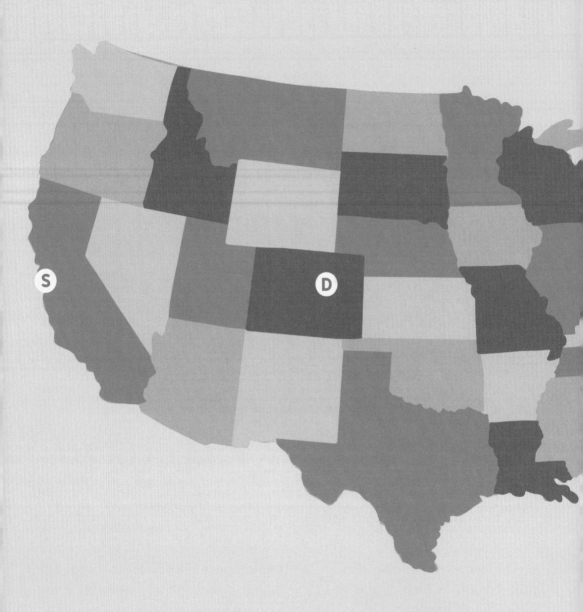

Coins are made at the United States Mint, which is also run by the government. There are **four** U.S. Mint locations that make coins:

DENVER, COLORADO

SAN FRANCISCO, CALIFORNIA

PHILADELPHIA, PENNSYLVANIA
(the largest mint in the world)

WEST POINT, NEW YORK

WHERE WAS IT MADE?

You can tell where a coin was minted by looking to the right of the big head of the person on the coin. There's a very tiny letter called a mint mark that tells you where it was minted.

D FOR DENVER
P FOR PHILADELPHIA
S FOR SAN FRANCISCO
W FOR WEST POINT

Coins used to be made out of silver and gold, which was really expensive. Today they are made out of copper and nickel alloys (mixtures, which are way cheaper).

All together, the U.S. Mint makes about **$28 million** in coins a year! **CHA-CHING!** By the way, my friend Noogie thought the Mint made mints. **LOL!**

DID YOU KNOW?

No matter how beat-up a dollar bill is, it's still good as long as both serial numbers are intact.

HERE'S WHERE YOU CAN LOOK FOR THE SERIAL NUMBER!

Old and damaged dollar bills are taken from banks to the Federal Reserve (a place where banks take their money . . . kind of a bank for banks) to be shredded, then recycled and made into compost, potting soil, and cement. There's even a recycling plant in Los Angeles, California, that burns shredded money to generate electricity. **WOW!** That gives a whole new meaning to "having money to burn"!

OLD MONEY GETS BURNED TO MAKE ELECTRICITY!

Moziah Bridges

At age nine, Moziah Bridges from Memphis, Tennessee, loved wearing bow ties, even to school. When he couldn't find any that fit his style, he started making his own bow ties with his grandmother's help. After constantly being asked **"Where did you get that bow tie?"**, he created the Mo's Bows bow tie company. Just a few years later, he was featured on the hit TV show *Shark Tank* and his sales blew up! With a strong work ethic and a never-give-up attitude, Mo has a net worth of over $1 million. He is listed as one of *Time* magazine's Most Influential Teens. Mo even signed a seven-figure contract with the NBA! *GO MO!*

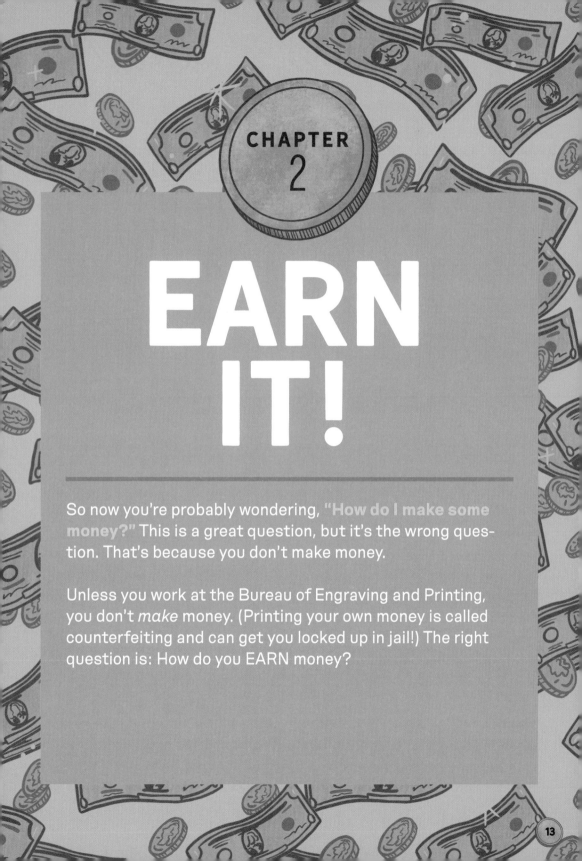

CHAPTER 2

EARN IT!

So now you're probably wondering, **"How do I make some money?"** This is a great question, but it's the wrong question. That's because you don't make money.

Unless you work at the Bureau of Engraving and Printing, you don't *make* money. (Printing your own money is called counterfeiting and can get you locked up in jail!) The right question is: How do you EARN money?

GETTING AN
ALLOWANCE

I remember the day like it was yesterday. My mom yelled, **"Kids, come downstairs. FAMILY MEETING!"**

Oh, boy! I thought. The last family meeting was about who ate the last piece of chocolate cake. Dad's eye is still twitching over that one.

Mom and Dad sat down me and my sister, Danielle, and said, **"Kids, we're going to give you an allowance."** We both erupted into cheers and high-fived each other. We thought that

meant that they were just going to give us money. Well, we were wrong. Then Mom said, **"We are going to give you a list of chores, and in return, we will give you each five dollars per week."** Danielle stood up and booed while I screamed, **"Awesome!"** Here was my first opportunity to work for some dough. My mom taught me a valuable lesson that day: You never get something for nothing. Anything worth having has to be earned. And my allowance was my way of earning money. **CHA-CHING!**

THE UPS AND DOWNS OF CHORES

UPSIDES

- $ Most chores are done at home.

- $ They're usually pretty easy and stuff you already do. Except now you get paid for it. *CHA-CHING!*

- $ If you have siblings, you can share and even trade chores.

- $ If you get really good at doing chores—or do extra chores—you can ask for a raise.

- $ You usually get paid in cash.

- $ **Your parents are the boss.**

DOWNSIDES

- $ Doing the same chores can get boring.

- $ You don't often make a lot of money with an allowance; your chances of becoming a million-aire via your allowance are *ZERO!*

- $ **Your parents are the boss!** *LOL!*

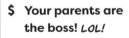

GIFTS AND TRADITIONS

We've all been there. You're about five years old and you take a bite out of an apple when . . . **OUCH!**

Your tooth gets wiggly. What's the first thing you think of? **TOOTH FAIRY!**

So it dangles in your mouth for a few days, then . . . pop! It comes out. You wash it off and put it under your pillow and go to sleep, and like magic, the next morning there's a buck or two under your pillow in place of the tooth.

Sure, it's awesome to get hooked up by the Tooth Fairy, but there's a problem with this situation: You didn't earn it. Uncle Earl always said, **"Anything worth having has to be earned."** Plus, you have a limited number of teeth.

Don't get me wrong. I can appreciate a few free bucks from the Tooth Fairy, Santa, Uncle Earl, or anyone else who wants to throw money my way. But there's nothing like working hard to earn your own cash.

Now let's talk about my favorite way to earn money, the way I became the King of Cha-Ching: entrepreneurship!

ENTREPRENEUR?
WHAT'S THAT?

It's simple: An **ENTREPRENEUR** is someone who starts their own business with the goal of making money.

LAWN SERVICE

TUTORING

$2 + 2 = 4$

PAPER DELIVERY

The key word in that definition is *someone*. I'm someone, and you're someone, too—**someone who has an idea!**

MY FIRST JOB

YES, SIR, JUST $5 FOR THE WALKWAY AND $10 FOR THE WHOLE DRIVEWAY!

My first job was shoveling snow. I was six years old . . .

On the first day, I made $55 in just two hours. *CHA-CHING!*

You bet I got back out there as soon as the next snowfall gave me the chance.

HEY, MS. JOHNSON! CAN I SHOVEL YOUR WALK FOR YOU?

After I finished, she gave me $5 plus a $5 tip. *And* she offered me a cup of hot cocoa and her famous chocolate chip cookies.

YOUNG MAN, YOU ARE A REALLY GREAT **ENTREPRENEUR.**

HUH?

ENTREPRENEUR: A PERSON WHO ORGANIZES AND MANAGES ANY ENTERPRISE, ESPECIALLY A BUSINESS.

Entrepreneur sounds very grown up. Except I'm not a grown-up. I'm just a kid. But a kid who is also an entrepreneur. What matters is that I had an idea, and I took action, and turned that idea into a business.

WOW, A NEW TITLE!

WHAT KIND OF **BUSINESS** WILL YOU **START?**

GREAT QUESTION! There are so many different ways to be an entrepreneur and earn money. Starting your own business gives you a feeling of independence. You control what you do, when you do it, and how you do it. Of course, to start your own business, there are a few things you need to figure out first.

GOOD OR SERVICE?

There are two types of businesses you can open: one that creates a **PRODUCT** (also known as a good) or one that offers a **SERVICE**.

A product, or good, is something you make or create. Lemonade is a product! Cookies and brownies are products. I have a friend who is awesome at making and selling jewelry. That's a product. I have another friend who likes to paint cool sayings on rocks. That's also a product. A product is a *thing*!

A service is something you do for someone, like wash cars, mow lawns, run errands, babysit, stuff like that. My job shoveling snow was a service. I already had a shovel, so I didn't even have to buy one. That means all the money I made was pure **PROFIT**! (I'll explain what profit is in a minute.)

Okay, now ask yourself: Would you like your business to be a product or service? Well, let me see if I can help you find the answer. Is there something you're really good at? I have a friend who plays piano. She's great at it. So great that she started her own tutoring business. Her business is called Susan's Rocking Piano Tutoring.

Can you play an instrument? If so, offering your talent to play at parties or even teach people how to play an instrument is a super service! Or maybe you're really techy or super into social media. Showing people how to use a computer or how to upload photos on Twitter is also a great way to start a business.

If you're awesome at something (playing piano), use your awesomeness to make a business. If there is a need (adults who don't know how to use Instagram), then offer your services. Although I do admit that enabling adults to join in the latest dance craze and then post their videos is super embarrassing (I'm talking to you, Mom). But if you can make a couple of bucks doing it, then go for it! CHA-CHING!

Not recommended: Pigeon walking, snowflake catching, squirrel chasing, snake charming, being a crash-test dummy, being a sparring partner for Laila Ali (technically also being a crash-test dummy)

SERVICES
Just to get your wheels turning, here are some services I brainstormed:

LAWN MOWING	SHOVELING SNOW	TECH SUPPORT
RAKING LEAVES	PET SITTING	DOG WALKING
TAKING CARE OF HORSES	BABYSITTING	WASHING CARS
BUILDING WEBSITES	PUPPET SHOWS	STAND-UP COMEDY
MUSIC LESSONS	FASHION CONSULTING	FACE PAINTING
HAIR STYLING	MANICURES	CLOTHING REPAIR

Maybe, on the other hand, you are really good at making stuff. Are you into sewing, building, or crafting things? Are you a great cook or baker? Personal chefs are in high demand. Do people really like what you make? Maybe your business is a product!

Check out the brainstorming ideas on page 23 to help you decide what kind of business you'll start.

Not recommended:
Lint sculptures, Swiss cheese parachutes, hamburger-flavored candy, tinfoil hats, mud pies made of actual mud, selling encyclopedias (look it up on the Internet)

PRODUCTS

Here are some cool ideas for products you could make and sell, just to get you thinking.

BAKED GOODS
LEMONADE, SMOOTHIES, OR OTHER DRINKS
ARTWORK
BEADED JEWELRY
ICE CREAM
BIRDHOUSES
FRIENDSHIP BRACELETS

DOG TREATS

TIE–DYED T–SHIRTS

TOYS

POPSICLES

PICTURE FRAMES

DOGHOUSES

KNIT SCARVES

MAKE A BUSINESS PLAN

SO, NOW YOU HAVE YOUR BUSINESS IDEA. How do you get started? Well, let me tell you, there's a reason they call me *Dan the Man with the Plan*. To do something as special as starting your own business, you need a well-constructed plan. In this case, a **BUSINESS PLAN**. A business plan is just a document that breaks down your big idea and helps you put all your thoughts in one place. I decided that my business would be a lemonade stand. It's fun and simple, and who can resist a kid selling lemonade?

Here's an example of my lemonade-stand business plan. (Don't worry, I'll get into the details about expenses and pricing in a minute.)

My Business Plan!

IDEA
A lemonade stand

NAME OF BUSINESS

DANNY DOLLAR'S ICE COLD Lemonade FACTORY

TARGET CUSTOMER
Patrons at large local events, like baseball and soccer games

MARKETING

Make flyers and signs, and use social media pages.

EMPLOYEES/ PARTNERS

Hire a minimum of two friends to help with stand sales and marketing. Pay $10.00 each out of total profits.

EXPENSES

Ingredients for about 100 servings (5 gallons) of lemonade, little umbrellas, marketing materials

PRICING

$1.50 per cup

GOAL

Make enough money to cover expenses for setting up the stand, pay myself, pay employees, and open another stand on the other side of town.

WHO'S YOUR CUSTOMER?

Knowing your customer is vital to your success. If I lived in Antarctica and tried to open a lemonade stand, I would probably fail big-time.

But in a place where the weather is warm, a refreshing cup of lemonade would be awesome!

BRRRR!

Think about where you live and what your community or neighborhood needs. **Here are some examples of jobs that fill a need in a certain time or place:**

Selling lemonade on a hot day 	Having a **babysitting service** during a town or community meeting
Mowing lawns in the summertime	**Raking leaves** in fall
Shoveling snow in the wintertime	**Styling hair** for a school dance 
Washing cars when it is muddy	**Making hot cocoa** at skating pond

Keep your eyes open for opportunities that fit the needs of the people around you, then fill those needs. People will thank you!

Can't think of a great business? Ask around. Talking to your parents, neighbors, and community leaders about the needs and wants of your 'hood could lead to a groundbreaking business idea.

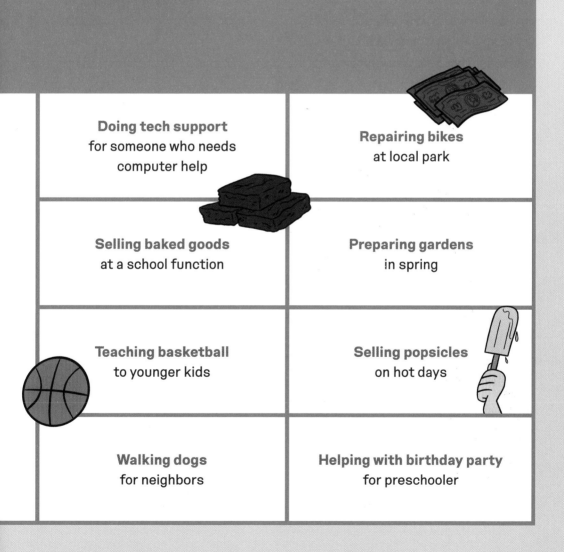

Doing tech support for someone who needs computer help	**Repairing bikes** at local park
Selling baked goods at a school function	**Preparing gardens** in spring
Teaching basketball to younger kids	**Selling popsicles** on hot days
Walking dogs for neighbors	**Helping with birthday party** for preschooler

HOW WILL YOU MARKET YOUR BUSINESS?

When you have your business up and running, will you keep it a secret or **SHOUT IT FROM THE ROOFTOPS?**

You'd shout it out loud because the more people who know about your business, the more potential customers you'll have! **MARKETING** is the art of spreading the news about your business. There are a ton of ways to do this.

Here are some marketing ideas that can be very profitable in the long run, but will cost you money:

Advertise on radio or in newspapers.	Give away samples.
Make T-shirts with your business name or logo on them.	Offer to donate a percentage of your proceeds to a charitable organization.

DREAM BIGGER!

In the marketing world, social media rocks! Not only should you have as many different social media accounts as your parents will allow you, but also make sure to have a hashtag for your business. This will help customers find you and connect you with like-minded businesses and organizations. My hashtag is **#DannyDollarKingOfChaChing.**

These marketing ideas are less expensive or free:

Print flyers.	Start a social media page.	Create a sign.
Create business cards.	Create chalk art leading to your stand if you're selling from a sidewalk.	Ask for referrals from satisfied customers.
Offer coupons.	Share images on social media of customers enjoying your product or service (make sure to get their permission to post it first).	

When it comes to letting people know that your business exists, you've got to be bold and creative. Think *outside the box*. The "squeaky wheel gets the grease"!

SPREAD THE WORD!

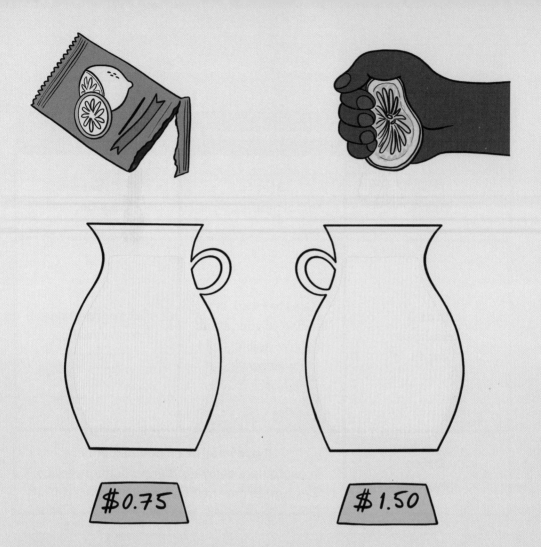

HOW MUCH WILL YOU CHARGE?

THIS CAN BE TRICKY! You obviously need to make a profit, but you don't want to charge so much for your product or service that you turn customers away. Here are a few things you can do to charge a fair rate and still make money.

RESEARCH: See what your competition is charging, and charge a similar rate. If you charge more than your competition, be sure you have a superior product. I use real lemons to make my lemonade, so I charge more than Cindy, who sells drinks mixed from powdered lemonade for 75 cents a couple blocks away.

WATCH YOUR EXPENSES:

Expenses are for things you have to buy to create the products you wish to sell. The less money it costs you to start your business, the more you can earn. My lemonade costs me about 46 cents per cup to make, and I sell it for $1.50. If I purchased more-expensive cups or spent too much on marketing materials, that would eat into my profits, and I might have to charge more money. We'll talk more about expenses and profits and how I got those numbers a little later (see page 38).

DROP IT: One of the oldest tricks in the book is to drop your price by a penny. If you want to sell your bracelets at $5.00, charge $4.99. Instead of selling your lemonade for a buck, sell it for 99 cents. Simply dropping a penny makes the customer feel like they're getting a better deal. Just be sure to have plenty of pennies on hand for change!

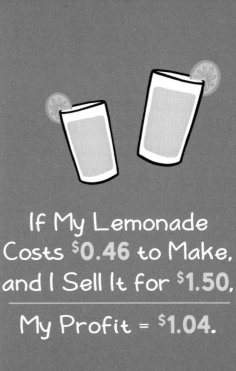

If My Lemonade Costs $0.46 to Make, and I Sell It for $1.50,

My Profit = $1.04.

If My Lemonade Costs $0.55 to Make, and I Sell It for $1.50,

My Profit = $0.95.

I will now make less money per cup.

WHAT WILL YOU NAME YOUR BUSINESS?

When it comes to creating and marketing a business, what you decide to name it might be the most important thing you do to separate yourself from the competition. A **cool and catchy name** will help you stand out and stick in the minds of your customers.

Which of these business names would stand out to you?

Danny's Lemonade Stand *or*

Mary's Nail Salon *or*

Tim & Tina's Snow Removal *or*

Susan the Piano Teacher *or*

The Bissells' Car Wash *or*

Think of a name that will make you feel proud and makes you and others smile when they say it. A funky logo doesn't hurt either!

WHAT'S YOUR GOAL?

Finally, having goals for your business is as important as having a plan. Do you hope to expand? Is there a certain amount of money you would like to make? Know what you're going to do with your money, then **do what Uncle Earl said:**

MAKE IT GROW!

NEED SOME
START-UP CASH?

Depending on the kind of business you're starting, you may need a little or a lot of **CHA-CHING** to get it going. If the business you want to start is a service based on your talent, like teaching others how to play piano, you may need only a few bucks for flyers and marketing materials. Your service isn't based on things you need to buy because your talent is the service.

But if your business is about making a product, you are probably going to need some start-up money. Start-up money is exactly what it sounds like: money to start a business. Another word for it is **CAPITAL**. If it looks like your business idea is going to need more capital than you can scrounge up, you might want to think about simplifying your business so that it's less expensive to get off the ground. You can always grow later!

With that said, if you need capital, it's no big deal. There are lots of ways to come up with start-up cash. **Here are just a few:**

Have a business partner, like a friend or a sibling, so you can pool your resources.

Borrow money from a family member or friend and pay them back out of your profits. When I started my first lemonade stand, my dad loaned me some start-up money.
DAD, YOU ROCK!

Ask your parents if you can **use supplies that are in the household already** (like old clothes for a T-shirt business or brownie mix for brownies).

Do you have old toys, games, or clothes you could **sell at a tag sale** or on sites like eBay? This could get you *CHA-CHING* and also clear some of the stuff out of your closet.

DREAM BIGGER
If you are going big and need some serious capital, look into online fundraising platforms like GoFundMe or Kickstarter.

HOW DO YOU MAKE A PROFIT?

If you want to stay in business and be successful, you're going to need to make a profit! Your profit is the amount of money you make after you subtract your expenses.

PROFIT

EXPENSE

Expenses

To make 100 cups of lemonade I need:

Water $0

➕

40 lemons $20.00

➕

5 pounds sugar $2.50

➕

100 cups $6.63

➕

Ice $3.00

➕

100 little umbrellas $8.65

➕

Marketing materials:
Chalk, signs, flyers $4.92

Total Expenses = $45.70

(To figure how much it cost me per cup, I just moved the decimal point two places to the left: $0.457. I rounded that up to $0.46 per cup.)

Take for example my lemonade business, which is **SWEET** . . . pun intended. To figure out how much profit I was going to make, I had to do some math. It looked something like the list on the right (and you can do your own math using the Profit and Expense Worksheet in the back of this book).

BY THE WAY, my customers love those little umbrellas! They're a cool marketing gimmick that **helps me stand out** against other kids selling lemonade. You can think of little gimmicks for your business, too.

ICY·ICE

LEMONADE

LEMONADE

CHALK

The day I opened my stand, the temperature outside was 87°F. I set up the stand at a Little League baseball game where there were hundreds of people (that's opportunity knocking!). I hired my two friends to hand out flyers and walk around with signs promoting my business (marketing).

Throughout the day, we were flooded with customers. We sold out of all 100 cups of lemonade. At $1.50 a cup, that's $150.00 in cold, hard cash! **CHA-CHING!** But that's not how much I walked away with. I walked away with $84.30. Why? Don't forget about the expenses. I had to subtract the expenses from my total to find out my **NET PROFIT**. That's the amount of money I made after all my expenses were subtracted.

See how I subtracted payroll, too? Noogie and Benjamin deserved a cut of the profit.

Net Profit

$$100 \text{ cups of lemonade} \times \$1.50$$

$$= \$150.00$$

$\downarrow$

$$\$150.00$$
$$- \$45.70 \text{ expenses}$$
$$- \$20.00 \text{ payroll}$$

(I paid Noogie and Benjamin $10.00 a piece for helping me.)

$$= \$84.30 \text{ in net profit for me!}$$
CHA-CHING!

PAY YOUR PALS

As an entrepreneur, it's essential to compensate (pay) your employees or helpers. They'll feel appreciated for their time and hard work, and maybe they'll want to help you out next time you need them. Take care of those who take care of you.

And hey, there was still plenty of money left in my pocket! With this much money, when I open my lemonade stand again, I won't have to borrow money from my dad.

OH YEAH!

ENTREPRENEUR ROCK STAR
Mikaila Ulmer

Mikaila opened her first lemonade stand in Austin, Texas, when she was only **four years old**. It was so successful, a local pizzeria asked her to bottle her delicious lemonade so they could sell it in their shop. Today, Mikaila is a teenage entrepreneurial rock star selling more than **360,000 bottles** of her Me & the Bees Lemonade in **1,500 stores**! CHA-CHING!

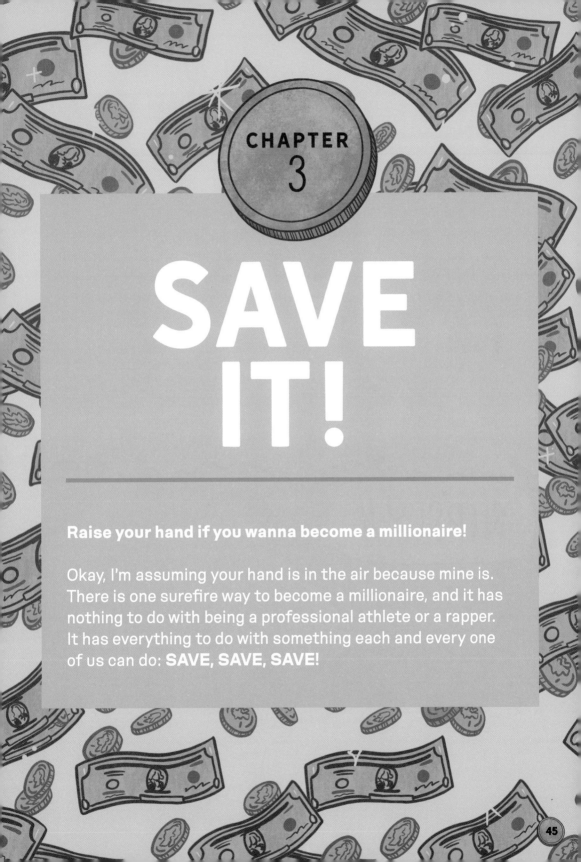

SAVE IT!

Raise your hand if you wanna become a millionaire!

Okay, I'm assuming your hand is in the air because mine is. There is one surefire way to become a millionaire, and it has nothing to do with being a professional athlete or a rapper. It has everything to do with something each and every one of us can do: **SAVE, SAVE, SAVE!**

WHERE DO YOU PUT YOUR MONEY?

Usually, for us kids, saving money starts with a piggy bank. While they are cute and fun when you're real little, piggy banks can end up being a bad idea. After stuffing Mr. Piggy with all the money Uncle Earl had given me, I had a little incident. My beagle, Nipsey, got hold of Mr. Piggy and buried it in the backyard. It took me three weeks to find it, but I also found out where our remote control, my mom's purse, and my sister's doll went!

Instead of relying on Mr. or Ms. Piggy, I'd like to suggest a much better place to put your **CHA-CHING**. Let me introduce you to my two favorite places in the world . . . **BANKS** and **CREDIT UNIONS**. To me they're like candy stores, except instead of sugary treats, they're filled with **MOOLAH!** *Ahhh.* I can smell the money just thinking about it. And the people there are cool. At my bank, Mr. Block, the security guard, always gives me a high five, and the bank manager, Ms. Anthony, always greets me with a **"Hello, Mr. Dollar."** Man, do I like the sound of that. She's the one who helped me open my first savings account.

DID YOU KNOW?

The idea of a "piggy" bank goes back to the fourteenth century, when Indonesian citizens stored money in orange-colored clay pots and dishes called *pyggs*. As time passed and cultures crossed, the pygg became associated with a pig, and it became a fun play on words.

After I deposit my money, I feel like a million bucks. Maybe because the more I save, the closer I am getting to becoming a millionaire!

CHA-CHING!
Let me break down the differences between a bank and a credit union.

CHA-CHING!!

BANKS

A bank is a **FOR-PROFIT** financial institution that helps you manage your money. Being a "for-profit" means that banks have **SHAREHOLDERS** (people who own stock in banks) who benefit from the profits of the bank.

CREDIT UNIONS

A credit union is a **NONPROFIT** financial institution. Credit unions don't have shareholders. Instead, they are owned by their members (or customers). When you're a member of a credit union, you actually own a small piece of the credit union. And because they're a nonprofit, they sometimes have lower rates on things like loans and higher interest rates on savings accounts. Which means more money for you! **CHA-CHING!** Whether you choose a bank or a credit union, both are great places to help you manage your money.

BANKS

$ For-Profit

$ Have Shareholders

$ Usually have more locations and ATMs

$ More likely to have advanced customer resources like apps and online technology

CREDIT UNIONS

$ Nonprofit

$ Owned by members or customers

$ May have better rates on loans and savings accounts

$ Known for having great customer service

OPENING A SAVINGS ACCOUNT

So, how do you use a bank or credit union? No matter how young you are, you absolutely should open a savings account. **If you're under 18 years old,** you can open a custodial bank account, which just means that a legal guardian (like a parent) and you are both responsible for the account. Generally, you can't make changes to the account without your guardian saying it's okay, but once you turn 18, it's all up to you!

Having a savings account ROCKS. Here's why you should take your cash to the bank as often as possible:

$ Keeping money close by in a piggy bank or under a mattress gives you easy access to all your cash. That's a big mistake. As soon as you hear that ice cream truck, you're grabbing a hammer to break open your piggy, then *POOF!* Your cash is gone. In a bank, your money is out of sight and out of mind!

$ It's a safe place, far away from curious beagles and desperate siblings. Your money is insured by the FDIC (Federal Deposit Insurance Corporation) or the NCUA (National Credit Union Administration). So even if there's a zombie apocalypse and cash-eating zombies eat all the money in your bank, you can get it back from the FDIC or the NCUA.

$ And the big reason why having a savings account rocks . . . (drumroll, please) . . . *YOU CAN EARN MONEY WITH INTEREST!*

IN THE BANK, YOUR SAVINGS ARE SAFE EVEN FROM CASH–EATING ZOMBIES.

WHAT'S INTEREST?

INTEREST is money that the bank gives you just for keeping money in your savings account.

WHAT?!

You heard me right! The bank actually gives you money for keeping money in their bank. It's not a lot of money, but it's more than you'd get storing it under your bed. Plus, the kind of interest you get with a savings account is *compound* interest. That means that if you leave your earned interest in the bank, you'll earn interest on that interest, too. **WOW, SWEET!** Let me explain.

Let's say because you really hustled and didn't spend money on silly stuff, you were able to save $1,000 this year. And let's say your savings account

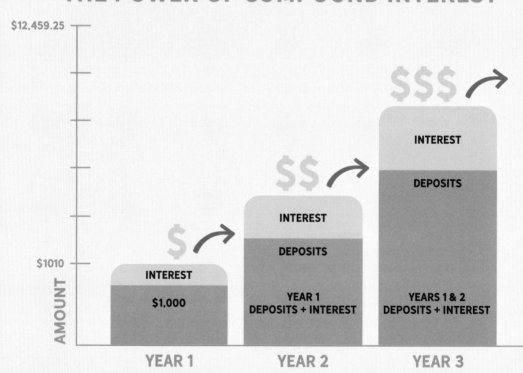

THE POWER OF COMPOUND INTEREST

$12,459.25

$1010

AMOUNT

INTEREST
$1,000

YEAR 1

INTEREST
DEPOSITS
YEAR 1
DEPOSITS + INTEREST

YEAR 2

INTEREST
DEPOSITS
YEARS 1 & 2
DEPOSITS + INTEREST

YEAR 3

$ $$ $$$

has an annual interest rate of roughly 1 percent. You find 1 percent of $1,000 like this:

$$0.01 \times \$1,000 = \$10$$

So, in one year, your bank would pay you $10 for that $1,000, turning it into $1,010. You earned an additional $10.00 without adding any more money. Now the bank will pay you 1 percent of $1,010. Awesome, right? But let's say after that year you really started saving your money and were able to deposit an additional $100 a month. In 10 years with compound interest you'd have $12,459.25 in the bank! $659.25 of that is interest—icing on the cake. And what's even more awesome about compound interest is that the sooner you start saving, the more you can make. **CHA-CHING!**

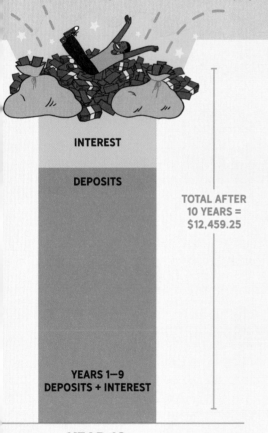

INTEREST

DEPOSITS

TOTAL AFTER
10 YEARS =
$12,459.25

YEARS 1—9
DEPOSITS + INTEREST

YEAR 10

DREAM BIGGER

Challenge yourself to see how much you can save in a month and beat that goal every month going forward. The more money you have in your account, the more money you can make in interest!

OPENING A
CHECKING ACCOUNT

If a savings account helps you save money, then a checking account helps you spend it. As with a savings account, you'll have to open the checking account with a parent or guardian. **Once you're 18,** you can operate the account on your own.

A checking account is a good place to put money that you plan to spend. It's smart practice to put the money you know you'll need soon in your checking account and the money you want to save for later in your savings account. Unlike a savings account, a checking account usually doesn't earn interest, but it can be super useful when you open your business. It will help you track the money that you spend as well as let you spend your money with a debit card (see the next chapter, Spend It!, for more info).

Checking accounts also let you write checks to pay people for stuff. In fact, someone might pay *you* with a check. When you get paid with a check, all you have to do to turn it into cold, hard cash or deposit it in your account is sign the back of the check. Then take it to your bank or deposit it using your bank's app on your mobile phone.

Margaret Johnson
123 Baker's Street
Somewhere USA, 10011

DATE 02/02/2030

PAY TO THE ORDER OF DANNY DOLLAR $ 10~00

TEN DOLLARS ONLY ———————— DOLLARS

FOR SHOVELLING SNOW

000000000 10987654321 321

WHAT DOES IT MEAN TO INVEST?

Investing is super important if you're going to become a millionaire . . . like me. Okay, I'm not a millionaire yet, but I'm going to be!

To **INVEST** means to buy something that is going to help you make more money. My first investment was taking the $84.30 I made from my lemonade stand and putting it back into my business, Danny Dollar's Ice-Cold Lemonade Factory.

I expanded on my flavors of lemonade. Instead of just having plain lemonade, I added flavors like cherry, peach, mango, and strawberry. *So yummy!* I purchased an ice crusher and sold lemonade slushies. My sales and reputation as an entrepreneur soared!

Then I decided that if I could make that much money with one lemonade stand, I could boost my profits with two, three, four, and even more lemonade stands! Now my investment has turned into a huge business with Danny Dollar's Ice-Cold Lemonade & Slushy Factories all over town, including in the local shopping mall.

DREAM BIGGER

Don't be afraid to expand on your product line by adding new products or services, especially if your customers are asking for them. Not only can expanded offerings add to your profits, they can separate you from the competition, making you a big deal in the kiddo business world.

INVEST BIGGER

I worked really hard to make my business successful and to earn money. Now it's time to make the money I earned work for me! How? Investing it in a **STOCK**, **BOND**, and other investment products. After all, the number of people who have become millionaires and even billionaires in the stock market is staggering.

Sure, investing in stocks and bonds sounds like a big, scary thing that only rich people in fancy suits do . . . you know, drinking cappuccinos with their pinkie out and reading some financial newspaper with their feet up on an expensive desk. *NAH!*

Anyone can invest money, and should! There are many different forms of investing, but let's start with what people most associate with it: **STOCKS!**

A stock is simply a little piece of a company. This means that when you own stock (or shares) in a company, you actually own a little piece of that company! *COOL, RIGHT?* When that company makes a profit and the business is doing well, the price on your stock goes up. You make money when you sell that stock for more than what you bought it for. For example . . .

A **BROKER** is the person who buys and sells stock for you, and they charge a fee for this service. Brokers are generally very knowledgeable about good and not-so-good stocks to buy. They can also help you when it's time to sell. You collect your money when you sell the stock. But it's your money, and the broker works for you. It's you who gets to decide what to do with your stock.

By the way, just like a bank account, you have to be 18 or older to buy stocks. If you're younger, you have to open a custodial account with a parent or guardian, just like you do with a bank account. You can also trade stocks online with brokerage companies like Charles Schwab and E*TRADE—same rules apply. They still charge a fee, though it may be less than the cost of going with an actual person broker. And you still need to be 18 to open an account (but you can open one with your parent or guardian). You can do this! If I can, you can, too. *CHA-CHING!*

You buy stock in the supercool ABC Sneaker Company.

You purchased the stock at $10 per share.

You purchased 20 shares:

$$10 \times 20 = \$200$$

Over time, the stock value increases to $27 per share.

Your 20 shares are now worth $540.

You made $340, minus your broker's fee.

INVESTMENT LINGO

Here are some investment terms you will need to know, so you can impress all your friends and family:

STOCK MARKET: The stock market isn't a place, and you won't need a shopping cart. It's simply a term used for the buying and selling of stocks.

WALL STREET: Wall Street *is* an actual place! It's a street in New York City that is a hub of world finance. It's also home to the world's largest **STOCK EXCHANGE** (a place where people buy and sell stocks) simply called . . . wait for it . . . the New York Stock Exchange.

BLUE CHIPS: No, you won't find these in the snack aisle. Blue chips are well-established stocks of well-established, often profitable companies. Disney, Apple, and Google are examples of blue-chip stocks.

DOW JONES: The Dow Jones Industrial Average tracks how the stock market is doing based on 30 large blue-chip companies, including McDonald's, Microsoft, and General Motors.

S&P 500: Like the Dow Jones, the S&P 500 tracks the health of the stock market, but it's based on the top 500 publicly traded stocks.

NASDAQ: The National Association of Securities Dealers Automated Quotations is a global marketplace for buying and selling stocks. It monitors more than 3,000 stocks from around the world.

LIQUID: An investment that can easily be sold or converted into cash.

The terms **BULL MARKET** (stocks going up) and **BEAR MARKET** (stocks going down) come from the way the animals attack. A bull strikes with its horns up in the air while a bear attacks by swiping its paws down.

BEAR

BULL

VALUE

TIME

PLAY SMART

Okay, investing sounds cool, right? Give a company some money, and get rich! **EASY PEASY!**

Well, hold on now! It's kinda not that easy. Investing comes with risk. Putting your money in stocks or any other type of investment (commodities, businesses, and so on) comes with the chance that you might lose some or all of your money when the stock values go down. **YIKES!** So it's important to only risk money you can afford to lose. Cashing out your savings and putting all the money in the stock of your favorite skateboard company could result in a wipeout if that company doesn't succeed.

So take it easy. There's a lot to learn about investing, but understanding the basics is not that hard. Not at all.

Like anything else, once you know . . . you know! And once you know, you can *do*!

All right, now you that you have the basics, you can go out and learn more! Here are a few tips to keep in mind:

$ It's a waiting game. The people who are successful in investing are the ones who are willing to wait years, sometimes even decades, to see if their stock makes them a lot of money.

$ Do your research! What's the track record of the company you want to invest in? How long has it been around?

$ Maybe invest in companies you know and like. Do you like social media? Then check out Facebook's stock price. Are you an athlete? Then maybe Nike or Under Armour is the stock for you. Into video games? Nintendo could be the one!

ENTREPRENEUR ROCK STAR
Benjamin Kapelushnik

When middle-schooler Ben Kapelushnik's mom bought him a pair of difficult-to-find LeBron James sneakers and a classmate of his offered to buy the sneakers from him, he got an idea. He asked his mom to buy him a second pair and used the money from the sale to buy and sell other specialty sneakers. Finding a creative way to tap into the sneaker market, Ben, a.k.a. SneakerDon, is now a powerhouse in the footwear industry. He has four employees and makes a six-figure income selling sneakers to celebrities like DJ Khaled and P. Diddy.

CHAPTER 4

SPEND IT!

My Uncle Earl once told me that there is a right way and a wrong way to do everything. There's a right way to hold a fork, to slurp a milkshake, and to ask someone to dance. I can rock the fork and milkshake thing, but the last one I've got issues with. But that's a story for another day.

He also taught me there's a right way to spend money. So I wanna pass along some of the things Uncle Earl taught me. For starters, know that you're in control of spending your money. **"I never accidentally bought anything,"** he once said. I like that. Every purchase is a choice. And I'm in control of my choices. *I'M IN CONTROL* . . . and so are you!

NEEDS AND WANTS

Spending money is a must! Why? Because we need stuff. We need food, clothing, and a place to live and chill. What we don't need is the most expensive item on the menu, a $200 T-shirt, or a 37-room mansion. We may want those things, but we don't need them. Needing is different from wanting.

A **NEED** is something you must have to survive!

A **WANT** is something you desire but really could live without.

For example:

We **NEED** clean air!

You might **WANT** a scented candle to make the air in your home smell nicer.

We **NEED** clean water!

You might **WANT** a fancy bottle of sparking H$_2$O with that Swedish name you always mispronounce.

Knowing the difference between a need and a want is superimportant to smart spending.

When you're about to throw down a couple of bucks on anything, big or small, ask yourself, **"Is this a need or a want?"** Deciding whether something is a need or a want can be tricky. Is a cell phone a need? Yes, it helps us stay in touch with our family and friends and can even assist us with things like getting information or directions to a store. But the newest and most expensive phone that costs more than a used car? That's definitely a want.

Now don't get me wrong. There's nothing wrong with WANTING stuff! We all want cool things. But there's a responsible way to get the things you want. I wanted to buy a bike so it would be easier to ride between my lemonade stands. Also, it's cool to have a bike. So I created a Fun Jar just for stuff I wanted, like a new bike! I took some of the money I got from my jobs, allowance, and gifts and put it in my Fun Jar! In just a few months, I was able to save enough to get a cool new bike. And what color bike did I get? Money green, of course.

WHEN YOU REALLY WANT SOMETHING, YOU CAN SAVE ALL THE MONEY YOU MAKE FROM JOBS AND OTHER STUFF TO GET IT.

WAYS TO PAY:
THE WALLET CHRONICLES

Once you've figured out whether you want or need that new skateboard or video game, it's time to pay for it. As a kid, you're most likely to pay with cash. But you'll see lots of adults whip out their wallets to figure out whether they'll pay with cash, a debit card, a credit card, or even electronically. There are **COOL** and **NOT-SO-COOL** aspects to each.

PAYING IN CASH

There's no age limit when it comes to using cash! This is the way I pay for everything. After all, I'm too young for a credit or debit card.

COOL: Almost everyone takes cash! Plus, using cash helps keep you from spending too much because once it's gone, it's gone. There are also no fees in using cash. *CASH IS KING! CHA-CHING!*

NOT-SO-COOL: Cash isn't traceable if you lose it. It can also be bulky and not easy to carry around, especially if you've got a bunch of change.

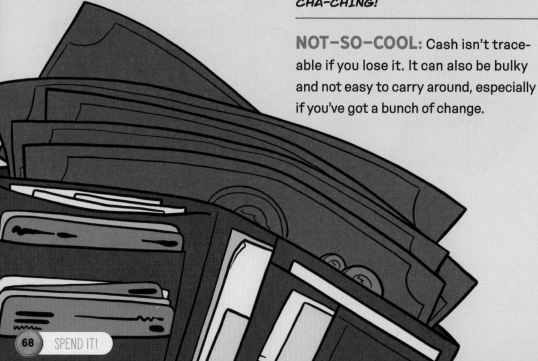

PAYING WITH A DEBIT CARD

To get a debit card, you must be 16 years old and have a custodial checking account. Your debit card is basically the money in your checking account in plastic form! Whatever loot you have in your checking account is what's on your debit card.

COOL: With a debit card, it's easy to get cash out of an ATM if you need it. Most businesses also accept debit cards. It's easy to track your purchases because the bank will show you a record of them. And because you use a PIN (personal identification number), a debit card is safer than a credit card if lost or stolen. Just don't tell anybody that PIN! Debit cards are great for online purchases.

NOT-SO-COOL: You may have to pay a small fee if you take cash out of an ATM that doesn't belong to your bank or credit union. And remember, if you don't have enough funds in your checking account, then you don't have it on your debit card either. If you try to take out or spend more money than you have, your bank may charge you a fee. That's the opposite of

CHA-CHING! Finally, there's a chance that if your debit card is lost or stolen, someone could make purchases without you knowing, but most banks have systems and safeguards in place to fix such problems quickly. If you know your card is missing, call your bank right away, and they will cancel that card and get you a new one.

PAYING WITH FINTECH

TECHNOLOGY IS SO DOPE! Tech companies have turned our smartphones and devices into digital wallets, giving us brand-new ways to pay for stuff. This is called fintech, or financial technology. You have to be 18 years old to use any form of fintech, but I'm psyched already.

COOL: Want a beverage from your favorite store? Use Apple Pay or Google Pay on your smartphone or smartwatch. Even Facebook Messenger allows you to send money to friends, family, or your favorite charitable organization. PayPal is another digital company that helps you buy stuff online and transfer money to friends and family. PayPal also owns Venmo, a popular mobile payment service. All these different apps make it easy for small business owners to get paid by their customers! These methods of payment are connected to your bank or credit card accounts, so they're easy to track and follow.

NOT–SO–COOL: You obviously have to have some form of tech to use fintech. Kinda hard to pay with your phone if you don't have a phone. Also, when you start your business, fintech companies take a small percentage of your sales for their services. When a customer pays with fintech, the money goes to the fintech company first, then the company takes their fee before they send you the rest of your money. This can take a couple of days.

PAYING WITH A CREDIT CARD

YOU HAVE TO BE 18 TO GET A CREDIT CARD. With a credit card, you're borrowing a financial institution's money to buy things. The financial institution makes money by charging you interest on your purchase if you don't pay them by a certain date.

COOL: Credit cards are super convenient. You can make small or large purchases without using your own money. And if you use your card responsibly, you can build up your **CREDIT**. This is really important for getting loans and borrowing money—people want to know they can trust you to pay up! A lot of credit card companies also allow you to earn rewards points and redeem them for gifts, free airfare, and even cash back. Credit cards are great when you are traveling and for emergencies. You can pay back the credit card company in small monthly payments (with interest).

NOT-SO-COOL: Because they are so convenient, credit cards make it easy to buy things you can't afford. A credit card can feel like free money, but it's not. It's money you have to pay back—with interest. If you can't pay what you owe on your credit card, or if you make late payments, your interest rates can go waaaaay up, from 0 percent to as high as 25 percent. *OUCH!* You end up spending lots more money to pay that interest, and what do you get? Nothing! It's also easier for hackers and thieves to steal and use your card without your knowing. If the theft is not reported quickly, the credit card company could hold you responsible for the purchases.

IF YOU GET INTO DEBT, YOUR CAR COULD BE REPOSSESSED.

WHAT'S THE PROBLEM **WITH DEBT?**

A credit card can be an awesome tool if used responsibly and a total disaster if used irresponsibly. Why? Credit cards can put you into serious **DEBT**. Debt is an amount of money (generally a lot) that you owe to a company or a person. If you have a lot of debt and can't pay it, the things you buy can be taken away from you. That's called **REPOSSESSING**. Thousands of cars are repossessed every year from people who get into debt and can't make their car payments.

Getting into debt can also affect your **CREDIT SCORE**. A credit score is like an adult report card that evaluates your spending habits. If you pay your bills on time and spend responsibly, you'll probably have a high credit score. With a high credit score, you can easily get approved by a bank or credit union to borrow money for large purchases like a car or a house, or to pay for college. Owing money on these kinds of things is okay as long as you keep making your payments on time.

If you use credit cards to buy lots of stuff you don't need and miss your bill payments, you may get a low credit score. With a low credit score, you could be considered "high risk." That means when you want to borrow money, financial institutions could either charge you a very high interest rate or deny you a loan all together.

It's hard to get your credit score back up once it has fallen, so it's best to have great spending habits from the get-go. Your future self will thank you!

CREDIT SCORE CHART

	720–850	Excellent (woo-hoo!)
	690–719	Good (all right now!)
	630–689	Fair (you're getting there)
	300–629	Poor (you've got work to do)

GET SMART WITH A BUDGET

One of the smartest ways to spend is to have a **BUDGET**. It's simply a plan you make for your money. A budget is important because it helps you keep track of what you're making, saving, and spending. And it helps you stick to your goals.

You've seen my business plan (page 26), and it's essential for keeping my business profitable. But my personal budget is just as important. It looks like this:

When I look at my budget, I know exactly how much money I have and where it's going. It helps me stay organized and accountable to myself so that I spend my money the right way.

I'M IN CHA-CHING HEAVEN!

My Monthly Budget

MONEY IN

$84.30
from my lemonade stand

THAT'S ALL PROFIT!

+

$20.00
from my allowance

+

$10.00
from Uncle Earl

Total =
$114.30

MONEY OUT

$50.00
to my savings account

WHICH WILL EARN INTEREST! ↑

➕

$30.00
to my checking account

➕

$20.00
donation to a charity

➕

$14.30
cash in my pocket
to use however I want

_____

Total =
$114.30

GIVE YOUR MONEY AWAY!

I know what you're thinking. This must be a typo! GIVE MONEY AWAY? Why in the world would someone do that? Now hold on. I don't mean to give it away to someone like my sister, Danielle. Nope, her I charge interest for borrowing my money. What I'm talking about is **DONATING** my money to support people and organizations that are trying to make the world a better place.

Uncle Earl once told me that giving is actually kind of selfish. I said that didn't make any sense. But then he explained. . .

He's right. Giving or donating makes me feel good, and it helps the organizations or people I'm giving to. It's a win-win situation.

Most people donate money to charities or nonprofit organizations that help a specific group. There are countless organizations that help all sorts of people and things:

Chances are, if you have a particular interest, like giving food to those who are hungry or saving humpback whales, there's a charity for it. The charities that I like to support are the ones that aid racial equality and justice. Last month I sent $10 to an organization that helps immigrants become legal U.S. citizens. Ten dollars doesn't sounds like much, but every little bit helps people in need. If lots of people support this cause, it could help hundreds and maybe even thousands of families establish a better life.

CAUSES YOU CAN SUPPORT WITH YOUR MONEY

- HOMELESS SHELTERS
- CANCER RESEARCH
- VETERANS
- COMMUNITY CENTERS
- RACIAL JUSTICE
- FOOD BANKS
- ENDANGERED ANIMALS
- NATURE CONSERVATION
- PET RESCUE
- *AND SO MANY MORE*

PLUS, DONATING IS A GOOD WAY TO GET TAX DEDUCTIONS. When you get older and start making enough money to support yourself, you'll also start paying INCOME TAX. You may be able to deduct your donations from your taxes. So donating doesn't just make you feel good by helping others, it can also improve your finances.

There's one other thing you can donate if you don't have much money, and it's one of the few things more valuable than money. No . . . not your Beyoncé autographed T-shirt. It's your time. You can spend a few hours volunteering at a local homeless shelter, senior center, or humane society. You get the exact same feeling of awesomeness by touching the lives of those who could use a little love. But if you're going to donate your time or money, make sure to let your parent or guardian know. Better yet, donate as a family! That's called **SOCIAL CHA-CHING!**

EARN MONEY

PAY TAXES

TAXES PAY FOR LIBRARIES, ROADS, AND MORE

DID YOU KNOW?
INCOME TAX is money that our local and national governments collect from everyone who has a job. Taxes help pay for the services that the government provides. This includes a ton of things, like building and maintaining schools, libraries, roads, and bridges. Our taxes also pay for our police officers, firefighters, mayors, and other government officials.

Joseph Cofer

When Joseph Cofer was 11 years old, he was already thinking ahead. He wanted to save money for a car, so he came up with a COOL idea: sell homemade ice pops at school functions. Little did he know how quickly his Schmancy Pops would start popping! Today he sells about 200 pops a day from his home with flavors like Key lime pie, chocolate peanut butter, strawberry, and pineapple coconut. He's even working on creating an actual Schmancy Pop store! He also donates a portion of his sales to help kids going though cancer treatments.

CHAPTER 5

DREAM BIG!

When I was getting started on my dream of becoming the greatest lemonade stand entrepreneur in the world (or at least on my street), I have to admit, I doubted myself.

I'M TOO YOUNG.

I DON'T KNOW WHAT I'M DOING.

BLAH, BLAH, BLAH.

Then I thought about some of my heroes. Steve Jobs, who created Apple. Oprah Winfrey, maybe the most important person in entertainment. And Barack Obama, the first Black president. I had to remind myself that they were all kids once, too! And I bet they had dreams of being great just like I do. *JUST LIKE YOU DO!*

YES, YOU CAN!

Think about it. At one point, Steve Jobs didn't know anything about computers. But he worked hard and dreamed big. At one point, Oprah didn't know about the media industry, but she worked hard and dreamed big. At one point, Barack Obama didn't know anything about leadership, but he worked hard and dreamed big!

Kids like you and me can accomplish the most amazing things, and it all starts by dreaming big and knowing that you can do ANYTHING!

UNCLE EARL ONCE SAID TO ME:

YOU KNOW WHAT'S THE BEST PART OF BEING A KID? THAT YOU DON'T KNOW ANYTHING.

YOU THINK THAT'S A GOOD THING?

Chuckling, he said, **"Definitely, Dan the Man. Not knowing anything also means you don't know what you can't do. You think everything is possible. Kids are always asking the most simple and important question in the world: WHY? Once you become an adult, you've heard** *no* **and** *no, you can't* **so many times you start to believe it. When you're a kid, you often ask, Why can't I? Kids are dreamers. They dream big. REALLY BIG!"**

And that's how I felt every time I hung out with Uncle Earl. Like a dreamer. *A REALLY BIG DREAMER.* He dropped a bunch of knowledge on me, which helped mold me into the world's greatest lemonade icon in the world . . . or at least on my block.

Sure, I'm just a kid, but I've learned a lot—from reading books, from my family, and from experiences. I've learned a bunch of things to become the King of Cha-Ching. I even discovered the secret to success!

WANNA KNOW WHAT THE SECRET TO SUCCESS IS . . . ?

YOU REALLY WANNA KNOW??
TURN THE PAGE . . .

The secret is . . . **THERE IS NO SECRET!**

DREAM *Big* & WORK HARD

THAT'S IT! People who have a huge imagination and take action to make their dreams come true usually succeed. There are a few other things I think it takes to kick butt in your field of awesomeness, and I'm happy to share them with you. I actually made a list of things to do to be the most awesome kid in the world. And I call that list . . .

DANNY'S LIST OF STUFF TO DO
TO DREAM BIG AND KICK BUTT IN WHATEVER YOU WANNA KICK BUTT IN!

GREAT TITLE, RIGHT?
DRUMROLL, PLEASE . . .

1. ASK WHY AND WHY NOT

When I started my first lemonade stand, my knucklehead sister, Danielle, said, **"You can't start your own business."** I asked her, **"Why not?"** After she scratched her head for a second she said, **"You don't know what you're doing."** I said, **"Maybe, but I'll figure it out."**

She didn't have a response.

DANNY 1 / DANIELLE 0

I earned $76.36 in sales that day! The King of Cha-Ching was born.

Whenever someone says you can't do something that you think is important, don't just throw your hands up in the air and give up. Challenge them. Challenge yourself! Ask yourself why *can't* you do a certain thing.

Don't let any excuse get in the way of your awesomeness! You really can do anything! *SERIOUSLY!*

Landing on the moon seemed impossible until Neil Armstrong did it!

Creating the cell phone seemed impossible until Martin Cooper, an engineer from Motorola, made it.

The idea of the Internet sounded ridiculous until computer scientists Vinton Cerf and Robert Kahn launched it.

So when you think of a business idea that may sound crazy to some but awesome to you, say to yourself, *WHY NOT!*

2. READ

One thing that most entrepreneur mega–rock stars like Warren Buffett, Oprah, and Elon Musk can agree upon is that reading is necessary to becoming successful. Why? Because reading is like jumping jacks for your brain! It helps with problem-solving, makes you smarter, and jump-starts your imagination. These things are key to getting you to the Land of **CHA-CHING!** Read at least 15 minutes every day to give your brain a work-out. Hey, lucky you—you're doing it right now!

What's also cool about reading, especially reading about famous people, is that you can discover what some of the greatest leaders ever have done to be successful. Wouldn't it be cool to find out how Beyoncé became such an icon?

How about learning what it took for Microsoft founder Bill Gates to create one of the most important companies in the world?

Or maybe discover the training regime of Simone Biles, who received the most Olympic and world championship medals in the history of gymnastics.

The secrets of the most amazing people in the world are just waiting to be discovered in the pages of a book!

3. GO PLAY

Playing is one of those things that doesn't seem to have anything to do with being successful, but think about it: When you're playing, you're being creative. You're putting your mind and body to work in a fun way. If you're playing with others, teamwork and leadership may be involved. Many board games and video games involve strategy. Playing is also a great way to kinda escape from stuff that may be bothering you. These are all things that are essential to dreaming big. Playing is definitely not just kid stuff!

4. SET GOALS

You can't hit a target that isn't there. In other words, you can't dream big if you don't even have a dream. Goals are the bull's-eyes of your dreams! And there are many different types of goals. Long term, short term, daily, weekly, monthly, yearly . . . you get the picture. My short-term goal is to have 10 lemonade stands across the city by the end of the year. My long-term goal is to become a millionaire investment broker who owns his own basketball team. Having daily, weekly, monthly, and annual goals will help me get there.

CHA-CHING GOALS

Here are my goals broken down into short- and long-term goals:

DAILY	$ Read for 15 minutes. $ Research cool stocks. $ Floss my teeth. $ Do homework.	$ Do 10 pushups. $ Eat two fruits and two vegetables. $ Get to bed by 10 p.m.
WEEKLY	$ Open my lemonade stand for business each Saturday and Sunday. $ Find other kids who want to open a Danny Dollar's Ice-Cold Lemonade Factory also.	$ Donate time to my local senior center. $ Work on my jump shot. $ Play board games with my family.
MONTHLY	$ Open one new lemonade stand. $ Create new lemonade flavors. $ Finish reading at least four books.	$ Deposit two-thirds of my lemonade stand money in my savings account. $ Make a donation to my favorite civil rights organization. $ Beat my dad at chess.
YEARLY	$ Have at least 10 new lemonade stands. $ Be able to do 50 push-ups in a row. $ Read 40 books.	$ Embarrass my sister in the Let's Dance video game (she beats me all the time). $ Deposit $2,000 in my savings account.

CHA-CHING! Some of my goals are about fun and just being awesome!

One thing you can do to remind you of your goals is make a vision board! My vision board reminds me of what I'm working so hard for. I'm not building my lemonade empire just to quench the thirst of my customers. I'm doing it for a cooler future for me and my family.

To create your own vision board, all you need is a few magazines, some glue, and a big piece of paper. (If you wanna be more techy, there are apps you can download to make really cool vision boards.) Cut pictures and words out that remind you of your goals, and glue them on the paper to make a collage.

MY VISION BOARD

Having images of your goals right in front of you can be inspiring!

ACHIEVED IT!

5. GET YOUR HUSTLE ON!

One of the many awesome things my Uncle Earl taught me is this: To be great, you don't have to be the smartest, or the coolest, or have the most talent. The most successful people are usually the ones who work really hard. Michael Jordan, the greatest basketball player ever (besides me), got cut from his high school basketball team and wasn't a starter when he got to college. But by the time he was a college senior, he was one of the most dominant players in the country and took his team to a national championship. The **GOAT** (Greatest of All Time) says hard work made the difference. Doesn't matter who you are or where you come from, hard work always wins.

6. LOOK FOR THE CLUES

I have the most awesome lemonade stand in the world, but I don't have the first! A gazillion kids have sold lemonade before me, and that's great because I can learn from them.

Cindy from the next street over uses lemonade mix instead of real lemons to make her lemonade. When customers had the choice, they chose mine! But when Michael opened his lemonade stand, he not only used real lemons for his lemonade, he also used ice cubes to keep it cold. **WHAT A GREAT IDEA!** I did the same thing, except I used shaved ice and made slushees. My sales skyrocketed. **CHA-CHING!**

Part of being awesome at what you do, whether it's throwing a fastball or starting your own business, is to learn from the successes and failures of others. They all leave clues!

FOUND IT!

7. TALK TO YOURSELF

When I say talk to yourself, I don't really mean have a conversation with yourself.

This kind of talk can raise eyebrows. What I do mean is to start using strong words to describe yourself.

One of my heroes is boxing champ Muhammad Ali. He famously said over and over again, *"I AM THE GREATEST,"* but he did that even *before* he became a boxing champion. He believed the combination of working hard and talking positively to himself was key to accomplishing his dreams.

The words *I AM* are so powerful. Whatever follows those words will help mold you into what you may become. Ever notice how someone who says *"I'M SO CLUMSY"* is always tripping over things? But the person who says *"I'M SMART"* gets an A on every test! Words have power. Use them wisely. (Why do you think I call myself the King of Cha-Ching?)

At least once a day, look in the mirror and say the words you want to become.

I AM THE GREATEST ENTREPRENEUR EVER.

8. FAIL FAMOUSLY

Some of my favorite entrepreneurs are failures!

What I mean is that every entrepreneur, leader, and success story has some form of failure in it. Like my Uncle Earl says . . .

> **FAILURE ISN'T THE OPPOSITE OF SUCCESS. *IT'S PART OF SUCCESS.***

I can't tell you how many times my lemonade stand barely made enough money to buy myself a cup of lemonade. But I didn't let it get me down! In fact, making a mistake, things going wrong, or just having a lousy day can fire you up to do better next time, especially if you learned from your mistakes. **Just look at this crowd of failures!**

FAMOUS FAILURES

$ **WALT DISNEY** was fired by his editor for lack of imagination! What? He only went on to create the greatest theme park in the world: Walt Disney World!

$ **HALLE BERRY** slept in a home-less shelter when she was a struggling actress. She said that her struggles made her stronger. Today she is one of the most famous actresses in the world and has even won an Oscar.

$ **OPRAH WINFREY** was fired from her first TV job because her producer said she was "unfit for television." Today she's a billionaire television icon.

$ **DO WON CHANG,** the founder of the Forever 21 stores, came to America from South Korea penniless and could barely speak English. He opened his first clothing store and named it Fashion 21, soon changing the name to Forever 21. It became one of the most popular clothing stores in the country with over 600 loca-tions. Today he is a multimillionaire.

What all these successful entrepreneurs have in common is that they all failed. But they didn't let their failures stop them from dreaming bigger and becoming entrepreneurial rock stars!

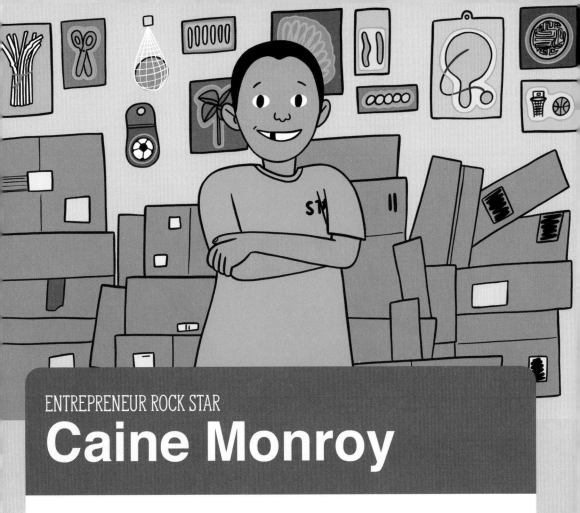

Caine Monroy

When Caine Monroy was nine years old, he created an arcade out of cardboard boxes in his father's used auto parts store during summer vacation. An entire summer went by, and he didn't have one customer, but he never gave up. He just kept making his arcade better. The next year, his first customer loved the arcade so much, he posted about it on social media—then BOOM! Customers came from across the country to play at Caine's Arcade. To date, Caine has raised over $242,000 toward his scholarship fund. Not only that, he sparked a project called the Global Cardboard Challenge and the website Imagination.org for young inventors, which has 750,000-plus kids in 80 different countries participating. WOW! See what a little imagination and a cardboard box can do!?

BELIEVE YOU CAN

There's a rock band that my mom loves called Journey. They have a song that my mom sings all the time, really loud:

DON'T STOP BELIEVIN'!!!

It's one of those songs that once you hear it, it's stuck in your head forever. And that's a good thing. Because we should never, ever stop believing!

My mom and dad tell me all the time, *"YOU CAN BE ANYTHING IN THE WORLD."* And they're so right!

In this book, we've read about adults who have accomplished the most

incredible things and kids who are just getting started on their path to *CHA-CHING.* And no matter the goal, no matter the idea, no matter what happens, it all starts with you! *YOU!* You are the most amazing force in the history of forces! You're like the Avengers minus the iron suit and that heavy hammer. And even though you can't turn green, your bank account can.

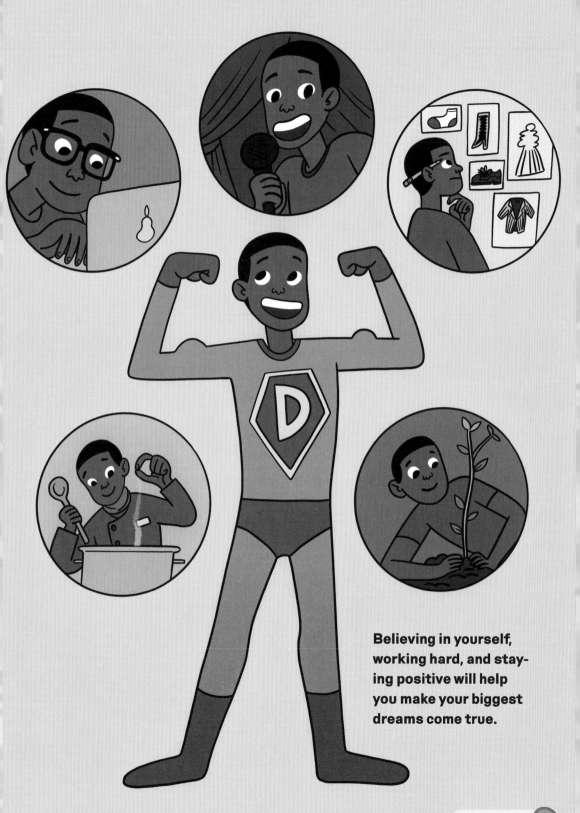

Believing in yourself, working hard, and staying positive will help you make your biggest dreams come true.

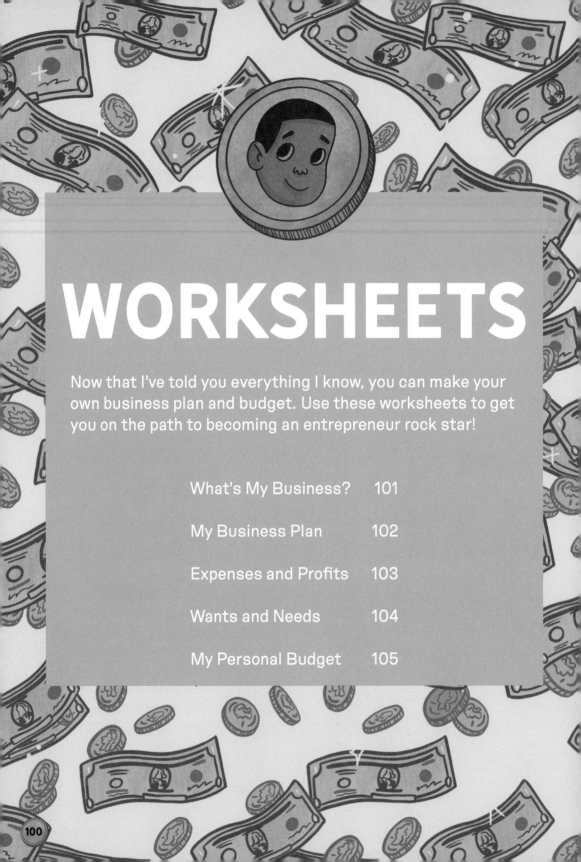

WORKSHEETS

Now that I've told you everything I know, you can make your own business plan and budget. Use these worksheets to get you on the path to becoming an entrepreneur rock star!

WHAT'S MY BUSINESS?

What are you really good at? Write down everything you can think of!

Is there something you make that's cool? Write down some cool things you make.

Look at your lists and pick the business idea you like the best.
Will your business to be a product or a service? Circle one!

SERVICE

PRODUCT

MY BUSINESS PLAN

IDEA

_____
_____
_____
_____
_____
_____

NAME OF BUSINESS

_____
_____
_____
_____
_____

TARGET CUSTOMER

_____
_____
_____
_____
_____

MARKETING

_____
_____
_____
_____
_____

EXPENSES

_____
_____
_____
_____
_____
_____

PRICING

_____
_____
_____
_____
_____

EMPLOYEES/PARTNERS

_____
_____
_____
_____
_____

GOAL

_____
_____
_____
_____
_____

EXPENSES AND PROFITS

EXPENSES	COST
MATERIALS	
OTHER	
MARKETING	
TOTAL	

NET PROFIT		
NUMBER SOLD	**× PRICE**	**TOTAL SALES**
	× $	= $
	EXPENSES	– $
	PAYROLL	– $
	NET PROFIT! *CHA-CHING!*	= $

WANTS AND NEEDS

MY WANTS

What do you want to save for?

MY PERSONAL BUDGET

Try making a budget to plan how you spend your money. It can be a weekly budget or a monthly budget—whatever works for you.

MONEY IN	
FROM MY BUSINESS	$
FROM MY ALLOWANCE	$
GIFTS	$
OTHER _____	$
OTHER _____	$
TOTAL	$

MONEY OUT	
DEPOSIT TO MY SAVINGS ACCOUNT	$
DEPOSIT TO MY CHECKING ACCOUNT	$
DONATION TO CHARITY	$
OTHER _____	$
OTHER _____	$
OTHER _____	$
CASH IN MY POCKET TO USE HOWEVER I WANT	$
TOTAL	$

GLOSSARY

BANKS ⇌ For-profit financial institutions that help you manage your money.

BARTERING ⇌ The exchanging of goods and services.

BEAR MARKET ⇌ When stock prices go down.

BLUE CHIPS ⇌ Well-established stocks of well-established, often profitable companies.

BROKER ⇌ A person who buys and sells stock for you.

BUDGET ⇌ A plan you make for your money.

BULL MARKET ⇌ When stock prices go up.

BUSINESS PLAN ⇌ A document that breaks down your big idea and helps you put all your thoughts in one place.

CAPITAL ⇌ Money to start a business.

COMPENSATE ⇌ To pay employees or helpers.

CREDIT ⇌ Money owed to a bank or business to be paid back in the future.

CREDIT SCORE ⇌ A scale, like an adult report card, that evaluates your spending habits.

CREDIT UNIONS ⇌ Nonprofit financial institutions that don't have shareholders but are instead owned by their members (or customers).

DEBT ⇌ Money that is owed to a person or a company.

DONATING⇨ Giving money to support people and organizations that are trying to make the world a better place.

DOW JONES ⇨
(Dow Jones Industrial Average) An indicator that tracks how the stock market is doing based on 30 large blue-chip companies.

ENTREPRENEUR⇨ Someone who starts a business with the goal of making money.

EXPENSES⇨ Things you have to buy to create the products you wish to sell.

FINTECH⇨ Financial technology.

FOR-PROFIT⇨ A company that has shareholders (people who own stock) who benefit from the profits of the company.

GOOD⇨ An item, like an apple, a pair of sneakers, a hat, a phone—a thing.

INCOME TAX⇨ Money that our local and national governments collect from income we earn.

INTEREST⇨ Money a bank gives you just for keeping money in an account.

INVEST⇨ To buy something that is going to help you make more money.

LIQUID⇨ An investment that can easily be sold or converted into cash.

MARKETING⇨ The art of spreading the news about your business.

NEED⇨ Something you must have to survive.

NET PROFIT⇨ The amount of money made after all expenses are subtracted.

NASDAQ ⇨
(National Association of Securities Dealers Automated Quotations) A global marketplace for buying and selling stocks.

NONPROFIT ⤳ An organization that uses the money it earns or raises to benefit social causes.

PRODUCT ⤳ Something you make or screate. Also known as a good.

PROFIT ⤳ The amount of money you make.

S&P 500 ⤳ An indicator that tracks the health of the stock market based on the top 500 publicly traded stocks.

SERVICE ⤳ A job that someone does for someone else, like babysit, clean teeth, build a house, or fix a car.

SHAREHOLDERS ⤳ People who own stock in a company.

STOCK ⤳ A little piece of a company.

STOCK EXCHANGE ⤳ A place where people buy and sell stocks.

STOCK MARKET ⤳ A term used for the buying and selling of stocks.

WALL STREET ⤳ A street in New York City that is a hub of world finance and the home of the New York Stock Exchange.

WANT ⤳ Something you desire but really could live without.

INDEX

FROM THE
AUTHOR

TY ALLAN
JACKSON

As a kid growing up in the Bronx, I was always working, except we called it hustling—hustling to make a couple of bucks any way I could. I washed cars. Ran errands for neighbors. Had a newspaper route. Anything to make money. AND I LOVED IT! Figuring out creative ways to make money was like a game to me. It was so much fun. While other kids were playing basketball or just hanging out, I was developing entrepreneurial skills that I still use to this day.

I never dreamed that my skills as a hustler would one day help me create a character who embodies the very same skills and mind-set.

The idea for Danny Dollar, also a kid from the Bronx, was conceived when my son was eight years old and he opened a lemonade stand. He made a whopping $50 in less than three hours! WOW! This prompted him to ask me, **"Dad, what am I going to do with all this money?"** And in my very fatherly voice I said, **"I don't know."** Well, my mother taught me that when you don't know the answer to a question, you can always find it in a book (like this one!). But when I went to the local bookstore to find a book to teach my entrepreneurial son about money, I couldn't find one . . . so I created one. And that's how my first book, *Danny Dollar Millionaire Extraordinaire*, was born.

Since then, Danny's story has been adapted into a theatrical play, appeared as a serial story in numerous newspapers, and inspired a foundation called Danny Dollar Academy. The book was even given as a gift to First Lady Michelle Obama from my hometown mayor. Now Danny has another book, the one you're holding in your hands, to give you even more info about how to start your very own business. Pretty cool, right? And supercool that Danny was born from a simple question from my son. It shows the power of what kids can do—and what they can inspire others to do! A simple question from someone as young as eight can change the world. I want you to think about that as you're reading this book.

As ideas float around in your head about money, developing a business, starting a career, and building your future, I also want you to think about how powerful and awesome you are! You really are capable of anything you put your mind, heart, and soul into. Absolutely NOTHING is IMPOSSIBLE. In fact, the word *impossible* broken down says I'M POSSIBLE!

Let's do this!

Ty Allan Jackson

MAKE A **BUSINESS PLAN**

OPEN A **SAVINGS ACCOUNT**

SPEND **WISELY**

ACHIEVE YOUR **DREAMS**

"So you want to be rich? And also, maybe, resilient, curious, patient, generous, and smart? This book is for you."
—CATHERINE NEWMAN, author of *How to Be a Person*

"Every kid deserves to grow up financially literate, and this book helps them do just that."
—JEANNINE GLISTA & JAMES MCKENNA, creators of *BizKid$* & authors of *How to Turn $100 into $1,000,000*

"A fun and necessary read."
—SIDNEY KEYS III, literacy activist & CEO of Books N Bros

START MAKING MONEY TODAY. NOW. That's right! Danny Dollar is here to help you start your own business and be an entrepreneur. Think up an idea, make a budget, calculate expenses and profit, and you'll be living the dream!

CHA-CHING!

TY ALLAN JACKSON is an award-winning children's book author, youth motivational speaker, and recipient of an honorary doctorate in humane letters. He is cofounder of the Read or Else movement and the financial literacy program Danny Dollar Academy. Find him at tyallanjackson.com.

Storey
www.storey.com

ISBN 978-1-63586-371-0

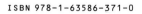

EAN
9 781635 863710
51295

JUVENILE $12.95 US